A Guide to
AMERICAN STATES

New Jersey

THE GARDEN STATE

AV² provides enriched content that supplements and complements this book. Weigl's AV² books strive to create inspired learning and engage young minds in a total learning experience

Your AV² Media Enhanced books come alive with...

Audio
Listen to sections of the book read aloud.

Key Words
Study vocabulary, and complete a matching word activity.

Video
Watch informative video clips.

Quizzes
Test your knowledge.

Go to **www.av2books.com**, and enter this book's unique code.

Embedded Weblinks
Gain additional information for research.

Slide Show
View images and captions, and prepare a presentation.

BOOK CODE

Q994148

AV² by Weigl brings you media enhanced books that support active learning.

Try This!
Complete activities and hands-on experiments.

... and much, much more!

Published by AV² by Weigl
350 5th Avenue, 59th Floor
New York, NY 10118
Website: www.av2books.com   www.weigl.com

Library of Congress Cataloging-in-Publication Data

Nault, Jennifer.
  New Jersey / Jennifer Nault.
      p. cm.
  Includes index.
  ISBN 978-1-61690-802-7 (hardcover : alk. paper) -- ISBN 978-1-61690-478-4 (online)
  1. New Jersey--Juvenile literature. I. Title.
  F134.3.N383 2011
  974.9--dc23
                              2011018522

Printed in the United States of America in North Mankato, Minnesota

052011
WEP180511

Project Coordinator Jordan McGill
Art Director Terry Paulhus

Photo Credits
Every reasonable effort has been made to trace ownership and to obtain permission to reprint copyright material. The publishers would be pleased to have any errors or omissions brought to their attention so that they may be corrected in subsequent printings.

Weigl acknowledges Getty Images as its primary image supplier for this title.

Contents

Located on the Passaic River and Newark Bay, the city of Newark has a population of about 280,000.

Introduction

Although New Jersey is a small state, it offers its citizens a rich blend of fascinating cultures, diverse regions, and thriving economic activities. New Jersey became known as the Garden State because of the excellent quality of its farmland. Today, New Jersey is also an important industrial state.

New Jersey has a long tradition of scientific and technical **innovation**. The inventor Thomas Alva Edison had his home and laboratory at Menlo Park. Edison, who held a record 1,093 patents, invented the phonograph, the light bulb, and the motion-picture projector. Edison and many others have helped New Jersey become a world leader in technology and communications.

The Delaware Water Gap National Recreation Area extends 40 miles along the border between New Jersey and Pennsylvania.

Princeton University enrolls nearly 8,000 students from all over the world. Today, it is one of the state's foremost centers for innovation and research.

New Jersey is rich in history. In the mid-1600s, the Dutch, the British, and the Swedish struggled for control of the region. During the American Revolution, more than 100 battles were fought on New Jersey soil. New Jersey was the third state to **ratify** the U.S. Constitution, and it officially joined the Union on December 18, 1787.

In the 1800s, New Jersey became an important transportation center. This allowed **industrialization** to spread across the state at a rapid pace. Today, New Jersey's cities are bustling with activity. Newark, located only 10 miles west of New York City, is the financial, trade, and transportation center of the state.

The sand and surf along New Jersey's Atlantic coast attract many people to the shoreline. Coastal Atlantic City beckons visitors with its 4-mile boardwalk, live entertainment, casinos, and amusement-park rides.

Where Is New Jersey?

New Jersey is located in the Middle Atlantic region of the United States. Except for a 50-mile border it shares with New York to the north, New Jersey is surrounded by water. The Atlantic Ocean lies to the east. The Hudson River separates New Jersey from New York City in the northeast. Pennsylvania and Delaware are to the west across the Delaware River and Delaware Bay. New Jersey's coastal location makes it an important arrival point for cargo ships.

New Jersey has long been an important transportation route between New York City and Philadelphia, Pennsylvania. New Jersey **commuters** can reach New York City by driving over the George Washington Bridge or through the Lincoln or Holland tunnels. Several bridges link New Jersey to Pennsylvania, and the Delaware Memorial Bridge crosses into Delaware.

More than 50 million vehicles a year use the George Washington Bridge to cross the Hudson River between New Jersey and New York City.

The New Jersey Turnpike is one of New Jersey's main highways, and part of it is Interstate 95, or I-95. The turnpike spans 148 miles with extensions. Another major north-south highway is the Garden State Parkway, which extends 172 miles, all the way from the New York state line in the north to Cape May in the south. Two interstate highways that span New Jersey from east to west are I-78 and I-80. The busiest airport in the state is Newark Liberty International Airport, which serves many passengers traveling to New York City.

Port Elizabeth was one of the first ports in the world to open a special facility for handling large cargo containers.

Mapping New Jersey

New Jersey has a total area of 8,721 square miles. Land makes up 85 percent of the total, and water accounts for the remaining 15 percent. New Jersey's Atlantic coast is irregularly shaped. Including islands, bays, and other coastal features, New Jersey has nearly 1,800 miles of shoreline, providing the state with one of its principal tourist attractions.

Sites and Symbols

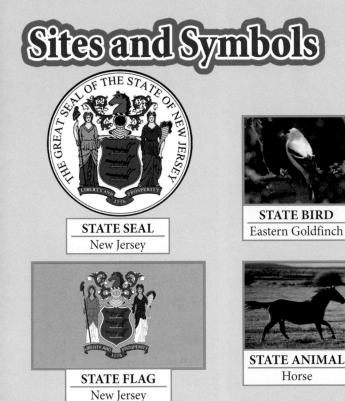

STATE SEAL
New Jersey

STATE BIRD
Eastern Goldfinch

STATE FLOWER
Violet

STATE FLAG
New Jersey

STATE ANIMAL
Horse

STATE TREE
Red Oak

Nickname The Garden State

Motto Liberty and Prosperity

Song no official state song

Entered the Union December 18, 1787, as the 3rd state

Capital Trenton

Population (2010 Census) 8,791,894 Ranked 11th state

LEGEND

— Road
— River
⭐ State Capital
• City
▨ New Jersey
— State Border

NEW YORK

Highland Mills · Yorktown

Suffern · Ossining

Ramsey · Stamford

Newton · Pompton Lakes · Paterson · Yonkers · New Rochelle

Stroudsburg · Hopatcong · Clifton · Passaic · Jericho

Belvidere · Dover · Madison · Union City · Levittown

Slatington · Easton · Phillipsburg · High Bridge · Newark · New York · Merrick

Bethlehem · Jersey City

Allentown · Somerville · Elizabeth · Bayonne

Kutztown · Emmaus · Flemington · Edison · Carteret

PENNSYLVANIA · Somerset · Hazlet · Middletown

Reading · Lambertville · East Brunswick

Doylestown · Princeton · Old Bridge

Pottstown · Lansdale · Hightstown · Eatontown · Long Branch

Phoenixville · Norristown · Yardley · Freehold

Bristol · **Trenton** · Asbury Park

Bordentown · Lakewood · Point Pleasant

Burlington · Silverton

Philadelphia · Mount Holly · Toms River

Upper Darby · Camden · Cherry Hill

Coatesville · **NEW JERSEY**

Kennett Square · Woodbury · Blackwood · Ocean Acres

Claymont · Glassboro

Wilmington · Hammonton · Tuckerton

Brookside · Pennsville · Collings Lakes · Egg Harbor City · Buena · Romona

Salem · Vineland · Pleasantville

Middletown · Bridgeton · Millville · Somers Point · Atlantic City · Ventnor City

Smyrna · Ocean City

MARYLAND · **Dover** · Sea Isle City

DELAWARE · Avalon

Harrington · Milford · Wildwood · Cape May

ATLANTIC OCEAN

Map Scale

0 — 50 Miles

N

STATE CAPITAL

Trenton has been the capital of New Jersey since 1790. The city, originally known as "Trent-towne," is named for New Jersey's first resident chief justice, William Trent. Trent, a merchant from Philadelphia, founded the town in 1719.

United States

Hawai'i Alaska

New Jersey

The Land

Although New Jersey is a highly **urbanized** state, it still contains a wide variety of natural habitats. Forests make up about 30 percent of New Jersey's land area, and farmlands account for another 10 percent.

The state consists of four distinct regions, which range from mountainous to marshy. The Appalachian Ridge and Valley region sprawls across the northwest corner of the state. East of the Ridge and Valley region is the Highlands section. Much of this section consists of gneiss, a hard rock that is formed under intense heat and pressure. Next comes the Piedmont region, which extends in a northeast-southwest direction across the heart of the state. This region is largely made up of sandstone and is the site of many of the state's major cities and suburbs. To the southeast, the Atlantic Coastal Plain covers three-fifths of New Jersey.

PINE BARRENS

Brendan T. Byrne State Forest and Pakim Pond are part of the Pinelands National Reserve. Established in 1978, the reserve covers about 1.1 million acres.

DELAWARE WATER GAP

In the Delaware Water Gap National Recreation Area, the Delaware River cuts through the Appalachian Mountains in northwestern New Jersey.

RARITAN RIVER

The Raritan River basin covers an area of more than 1,100 square miles, from central New Jersey to Raritan Bay.

CAPE MAY

Cape May is a peninsula and seaside resort at the state's southern tip, where Delaware Bay meets the Atlantic Ocean.

In January 2011, Newark Liberty International Airport received a record monthly total of more than 3 feet of snow.

Climate

I n the summer, tropical air currents from the ocean can result in hot and humid conditions. The average temperature in July ranges from 70° F in the north to 76° F in the southwest. In January mild ocean currents moderate the climate, keeping the average temperature at about 31° F. Average annual precipitation ranges from less than 40 inches at Atlantic City, on the Jersey shore, to more than 53 inches in Morris Plains, in the north-central part of the state.

The weather has an enormous effect on tourism in the state. Shore communities hope for warm, sunny summer weekends, with little rain to discourage beach crowds.

Average Annual Temperatures Across New Jersey

Temperatures at High Point are generally cooler than at other places in New Jersey. Why is this so?

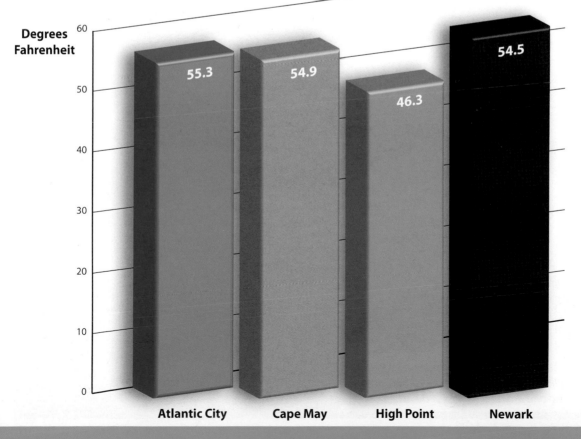

Degrees Fahrenheit

Atlantic City	Cape May	High Point	Newark
55.3	54.9	46.3	54.5

Natural Resources

Coastal waters supply New Jersey's fishing industry with clams, crabs, squid, flounder, mackerels, menhaden, oysters, and swordfish. Overfishing of lobsters, scallops, and tuna has reduced the catch of these species.

The construction industry, which contributes more than $16 billion annually to the New Jersey economy, relies on sand and gravel produced in the state.

The harvest season for fresh New Jersey strawberries usually runs from late May through June.

New Jersey's Department of Environmental Protection was formed on Earth Day in 1970. It is responsible for protecting plants and animals in New Jersey, as well as maintaining water and air quality.

In rural areas, roadside stands sell fresh Jersey tomatoes, sweet corn, and other local crops.

Most trees in New Jersey are too small to be used for lumber. Some are used to make wood pulp.

The state's six main fishing ports are Belford, Point Pleasant, Barnegat Light, Atlantic City, Cape May, and Port Norris. In the 1970s, Barnegat Light promoted itself as the "tilefish capital of the world."

During the American Revolution, northern New Jersey was an important source of iron ore. Today, however, only a few minerals are mined in the state. The most important of these include basalt, sand, gravel, clay, and greensand marl, which is used as fertilizer and to remove minerals from well water.

Early settlers relied on the state's soils for a living. When industrialization spread across New Jersey in the 1800s, manufacturing replaced agriculture as the state's main source of income. Still, New Jersey has thousands of farms, most of which are run by families.

Plants

Forests cover nearly one-third of New Jersey. Woodlands in the northern part of the state contain hickory, oak, red maple, and hemlock trees. Less hardy trees grow closer to the Atlantic Coastal Plain. These include scrub oak, pitch pine, and white cedar. The oak is the most common tree in the forests of northern New Jersey. The state's oak trees were once used in shipbuilding.

Many flowers flourish in the state, including honeysuckles, goldenrods, azaleas, buttercups, and Queen Anne's lace.

VIOLET

The New Jersey legislature voted to make the violet the state flower during 1913–1914. Long after that law lapsed, a new state law in 1971 restored the violet to its place of honor.

RED OAK

Green in summer, the leaves of the red oak tree turn reddish brown when autumn comes.

AZALEA

Hundreds of different varieties of azaleas can flourish in New Jersey soil.

QUEEN ANNE'S LACE

A member of the carrot family, Queen Anne's lace is a wildflower that grows up to 4 feet tall.

The red oak is New Jersey's state tree. It was adopted in 1950.

The dogwood has been named as the state's official memorial tree.

New Jersey's state flower is officially known as the common meadow violet.

Goldenrod grows wild in much of new Jersey and is regarded as a weed by blueberry and Christmas tree growers. The plant is pollinated by insects seeking nectar from the golden flowers.

Animals

New Jersey is home to a wide variety of animals. There are about 90 species of mammals and 80 species of reptiles and amphibians. Common animals found in the state include otter, muskrat, opossum, rabbit, deer, mink, skunk, and raccoon. Black bears had become scarce in New Jersey because of overhunting and habitat loss, but protective measures have boosted their numbers.

New Jersey's woodlands and wetlands attract some 325 species of birds. Near the shores of the Atlantic Ocean, wild ducks and geese are common. Hawks, ruffed grouse, quails, wild turkeys, partridges, and pheasants live in the state's forests and meadows. **Endangered species** in New Jersey include the bobcat and Allegheny woodrat. Many bird and reptile species are also endangered or threatened.

BOBCAT

Bobcats nearly became extinct in New Jersey when their forest habitat was cut down. Since 1991, state law has protected them as an endangered species.

WOOD DUCKS

Wood ducks are plentiful in the swamplands of northern New Jersey.

The horse became New Jersey's state animal in 1977.

Migrating birds may find sanctuary at Edwin B. Forsythe National Wildlife Refuge.

Island Beach, a state park, has more than 3,000 acres of plant and animal life. The park is known for its sandy coastal dunes and tidal marshes.

Rare birds can be found at the Cape May Bird Observatory. This facility is one of the top bird-watching spots in North America.

The brook trout is New Jersey's official state fish.

The Marine Mammal Stranding Center, based in Brigantine, saves stranded dolphins, whales, sea turtles, and seals.

New Jersey's state bird is the eastern goldfinch. This little yellow bird will sometimes remain in New Jersey throughout the winter.

RABBITS

Rabbits can thrive in woodlands, wetlands, and even on suburban lawns.

BLACK BEAR

The black bear is the largest land mammal that is native to the state. It is seen most often in the forested areas of northwestern New Jersey.

Tourism

With numerous resorts strung along the Atlantic coastline, tourism plays an important role in New Jersey's economy. Atlantic City is one of New Jersey's most popular destinations. Long known for its sandy beaches, Atlantic City also offers its famous wooden boardwalk, amusement-park rides, luxury hotels, nightclubs, and gambling casinos.

Many New Jersey cities contain historic buildings and majestic homes that date back to the 1700s. Visitors can step back in time by touring the William Trent House in Trenton. Another popular historic site is Thomas Alva Edison's laboratory at Thomas Edison National Historical Park in West Orange. Here Edison invented the motion-picture camera and an electric storage battery, as well as an improved design for the phonograph. The laboratory remains exactly as Edison left it.

ATLANTIC CITY

Atlantic City's hotels and casinos attract about 34 million visitors each year.

MENLO PARK

The Edison Tower honors the inventor who developed the light bulb. Built in 1937, the tower is now being restored.

BALLOON FESTIVAL

Hot-air balloonists from all over the United States flock to Readington each year for a three-day festival.

JERSEY SHORE

Vacationers increase the population of Bradley Beach from 5,000 to 30,000 at the height of the summer tourist season.

The game of Monopoly was originally based on the streets of Atlantic City.

Morristown National Historical Park is located in the area where the Continental Army, headed by George Washington, made its winter headquarters during the American Revolution.

Lucy the Elephant, a 65-foot-tall elephant constructed in 1881, guards Margate Beach. Lucy was made out of wood and then covered with sheet metal.

Ocean City has become one of New Jersey's most popular family resorts, with a boardwalk that extends 2.5 miles.

The first Miss America pageant was held in Atlantic City in 1921.

Industry

Industry has long been central to New Jersey's economy. In the 1700s, New Jerseyans were known for glass blowing and iron forging. New manufacturing industries developed after Alexander Hamilton organized the Society for Establishing Useful Manufactures in 1791. The society founded the city of Paterson, which became known for its cotton mills, locomotives, silk, linens, and revolvers. Newark became noted for leather tanning, jewelry, and shoe manufacturing. In the 20th century, New Jersey emerged as a leader in technology, communications, and research.

Industries in New Jersey
Value of Goods and Services in Millions of Dollars

Many industries are important to the economy of New Jersey. What benefits does New Jersey gain from having a diverse economy instead of concentrating on only one or two industries?

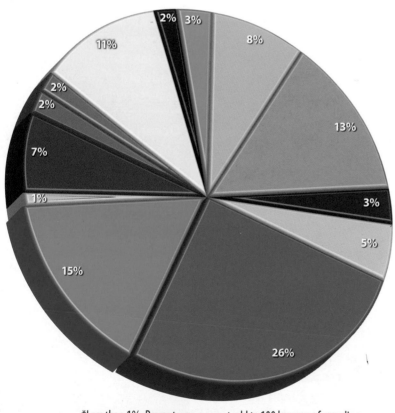

LEGEND

*	Agriculture, Forestry, and Fishing	$758
*	Mining	$66
■	Utilities	$7,995
■	Construction	$16,345
■	Manufacturing	$38,591
■	Wholesale and Retail Trade	$64,296
■	Transportation	$14,056
■	Media and Entertainment	$26,102
■	Finance, Insurance, and Real Estate	$126,482
■	Professional and Technical Services	$72,572
■	Education	$4,745
■	Health Care	$35,754
■	Hotels and Restaurants	$11,216
■	Other Services	$10,221
■	Government	$53,767

TOTAL $482,967

*Less than 1%. Percentages may not add to 100 because of rounding.

The Great Falls of the Passaic River, which provided power for Paterson's early industries, is now part of Great Falls State Park.

Despite being heavily urbanized, New Jersey has always had an important agricultural sector. The state is among the nation's leading producers of blueberries, cranberries, and peaches. Cranberries thrive in the marshlands of the Atlantic Coastal Plain. Cranberry farmers flood their fields with water and use water reels to shake off ripened berries. They then collect the floating berries into trucks. Other fruits grown in New Jersey include apples and strawberries. The state's main field crops are soybeans, corn, and hay.

New Jersey has about 3,500 acres of cranberry bogs.

Goods and Services

New Jersey is the country's leading producer of chemicals and **pharmaceuticals**. The state has earned the nickname "The Nation's Medicine Chest" because its pharmaceutical companies develop about one-third of the medicines approved by the U.S. Food and Drug Administration. New Jersey is the national or global headquarters for many well-known pharmaceutical companies, including Johnson & Johnson, Merck, and Bristol-Myers Squibb. Other important goods that come from the state are machinery, instruments, clothing, and electrical products.

Many of New Jersey's workers are employed in the service sector. Service-related jobs include working in hotels, gas stations, restaurants, schools, and hospitals. The majority of jobs in tourism are concentrated in the resorts along the Atlantic coast.

Each year, pharmaceutical firms add about $30 billion to New Jersey's economy.

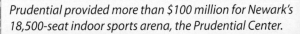

Prudential provided more than $100 million for Newark's 18,500-seat indoor sports arena, the Prudential Center.

With so many people living in New Jersey, real estate is a key sector of the economy. The state is also home to many insurance and financial services companies. Prudential, one of the world's largest life-insurance companies, has its headquarters in Newark.

New Jersey is the site of Princeton University and Rutgers, the State University of New Jersey, two of the nation's oldest and most respected universities. Princeton is the fourth-oldest university in the country. U.S. Presidents James Madison and Woodrow Wilson and Vice Presidents Aaron Burr and George M. Dallas were all educated at Princeton. More than two dozen Princeton faculty and graduates have received Nobel Prizes. Among them are Woodrow Wilson, who won the Nobel Prize for Peace in 1919, and Toni Morrison, who won the Nobel Prize for Literature in 1993. Rutgers is the eighth-oldest university in the country and enrolls more than 50,000 students annually.

The pharmaceutical industry in New Jersey provides jobs for about 60,000 people.

The first drive-in movie theater in the country was built in Camden in 1933.

In 1883, Roselle became the first town in the United States to receive electricity.

The first regularly scheduled steamboat ferry service in the United States was established in 1811 between New York City and Hoboken.

The state's first newspaper was the *New Jersey Gazette*. The newspaper began publishing in 1777 in Trenton.

Rutgers University was founded in 1766 as Queens College by the Dutch Reformed Church. Its main campus is in New Brunswick, and it has branch campuses in Newark and Camden.

New Jersey has more than 50 universities and colleges.

American Indians

New Jersey was first inhabited at least 10,000 years ago. **Archaeologists** believe that the **prehistoric** Indians of the region hunted mammoths and other large animals. Over the next several thousand years, other American Indian groups resided on the land that is now New Jersey.

The Lenape Indians pledged to live in peace with the Europeans who arrived in the New Jersey region.

By the time the first European explorers arrived in the 1500s, New Jersey was inhabited by Algonquian-speaking Indians. Europeans called them Delaware Indians, but they called themselves the Lenape, or Lenni Lenape, which means "original people." The Lenape relied primarily on agriculture, using ashes from burned trees as fertilizer to help crops grow. They also hunted and fished for food. The Lenape lived in longhouses made of young saplings and covered in tree bark.

Between 10,000 and 20,000 Lenape lived in the area at the time of contact with Europeans, but new diseases brought by the Europeans devastated the Indians. Without **immunity** to these diseases, many Lenape died. By the 1800s, most of the remaining Lenape had left New Jersey. Several thousand **descendants** of the Lenape now live in Oklahoma, Wisconsin, and the Canadian province of Ontario.

Woolly mammoths roamed New Jersey in prehistoric times but disappeared after the last Ice Age.

A full-size replica of the Half Moon commemorates the 1609 voyage in which Henry Hudson sailed from the Netherlands to the New World.

Explorers

I n 1498, John Cabot became the first European to see the New Jersey coast. Cabot was an Italian **navigator** and explorer who was funded by the English. Not until 1524 was the New Jersey coast explored and charted by Giovanni da Verrazzano. Verrazzano, who was also Italian but sailed to North America under the French flag, paused his journey to anchor his ship off Sandy Hook.

In 1609, a Dutch-owned ship called the *Half Moon* carried the English explorer Henry Hudson and his sailors to New Jersey. Hudson claimed the territory for the Dutch, calling it New Netherland, and explored the land extensively. Dutch settlements soon began to spring up across the region.

Timeline of Settlement

Early Exploration

1498 Italian navigator John Cabot sails past the New Jersey coast.

1524 Giovanni da Verrazzano explores coastal New Jersey.

1609 Henry Hudson enters Newark Bay and claims the region for the Dutch.

First Colonies Established

1660 The Dutch establish a permanent settlement at Bergen, now Jersey City.

1664 The Dutch, led by Peter Stuyvesant, surrender control of the region to the English.

Further Settlement

1719 William Trent founds Trent-towne, which later becomes Trenton, New Jersey's capital.

1746 Princeton University is founded as a college in Elizabeth. It moves to its current location in 1756.

American Revolution and Civil War

1775–1783 During the American Revolution, New Jersey is the site of more than 100 battles.

1787 On December 18, New Jersey becomes the third state to join the Union.

1861–1865 New Jersey sides with the Union during the Civil War.

Early Settlers

T he Dutch established trading settlements at several spots along the coast, including the sites of present-day Hoboken and Jersey City. Beginning in 1638, Swedish traders built trading forts on the east bank of the Delaware River. In 1655, the Dutch, under the leadership of Peter Stuyvesant, drove out the Swedish traders.

Map of Settlements and Resources in Early New Jersey

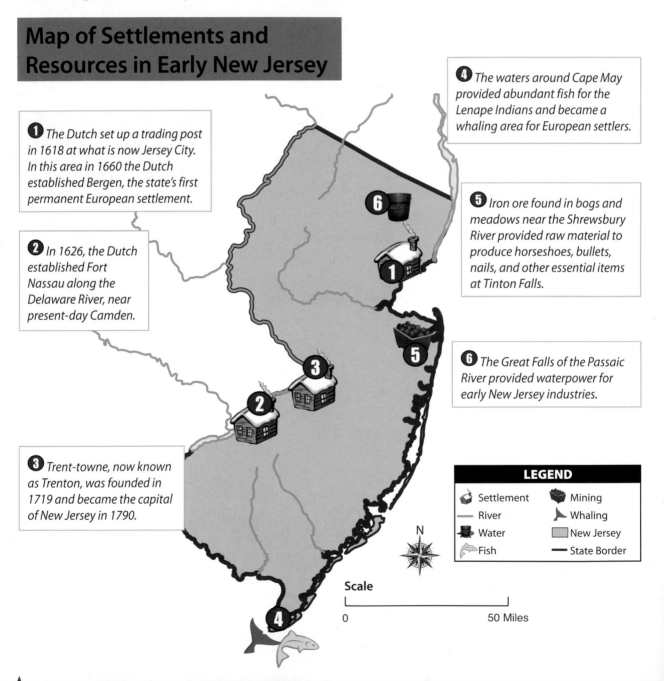

❶ The Dutch set up a trading post in 1618 at what is now Jersey City. In this area in 1660 the Dutch established Bergen, the state's first permanent European settlement.

❷ In 1626, the Dutch established Fort Nassau along the Delaware River, near present-day Camden.

❸ Trent-towne, now known as Trenton, was founded in 1719 and became the capital of New Jersey in 1790.

❹ The waters around Cape May provided abundant fish for the Lenape Indians and became a whaling area for European settlers.

❺ Iron ore found in bogs and meadows near the Shrewsbury River provided raw material to produce horseshoes, bullets, nails, and other essential items at Tinton Falls.

❻ The Great Falls of the Passaic River provided waterpower for early New Jersey industries.

LEGEND
🪣 Settlement		🌹 Mining	
— River		⚓ Whaling	
🎩 Water		▨ New Jersey	
🐟 Fish		▬ State Border	

N

Scale

0   50 Miles

In 1664, the English claimed the area for themselves. The English based their claim on the earlier voyage of Cabot and backed it up with their mighty naval forces. The Dutch surrendered New Netherland to the English without a fight. The English renamed the region New Jersey and began to sell off land to settlers at low prices. New Jersey shared an English royal governor with New York until 1738, when New Jersey was given its own governor.

During the 1600s and 1700s, religious freedom developed in New Jersey. The Quakers benefited from this policy. Founded in England, the Quakers were a religious group that rejected traditional forms of worship and relied instead upon silent meditation. They followed a simple life and wore plain clothing. They were often **persecuted** for their beliefs.

When the Quakers arrived in New Jersey, they were relieved to find a place where they could practice their religion freely. Different groups looking for religious and political freedom soon followed. Many early settlers lived a rural farming life.

Blacksmiths made tools using metal refined from iron ore mined in New Jersey.

I DIDN'T KNOW THAT!

Early explorers called the New Jersey region "the northeast territory."

Cape May is named after the Dutch explorer Cornelius Mey, or May. who explored the Delaware Bay region in the early 1600s.

Roman Catholic missionaries arrived in New Jersey as early as 1672.

The colony of New Jersey changed hands several times. After the English took the land from the Dutch in 1664, King Charles II gave it to his brother James, the duke of York. Next, the duke of York divided the land in two and gave control of half to Lord John Berkeley and control of the other half to Sir George Carteret. Lord Berkeley sold his share to the Quakers in 1674.

In 1676 the Quintipartite Deed split New Jersey in two, forming East Jersey and West Jersey. Sir George Carteret headed East Jersey, while the Quakers ran West Jersey. New Jersey was reunited in 1702.

Swedish settlers in New Jersey built the first log cabin in the United States.

Notable People

With its large and diverse population, New Jersey has been home to many notable people, ranging from pop stars to presidents. The founder of the American Red Cross lived in the state, as did one of the world's greatest inventors. One famous New Jerseyan was both a basketball star and a popular politician, while another has made a name for himself with his sharp-tongued comedy.

**CLARA BARTON
(1821–1912)**

Born in Massachusetts, Clara Barton became a teacher and nurse. In the early 1850s she began teaching in Bordentown, New Jersey, where she founded one of the first free public schools in the state. Later, during the Civil War, she nursed injured Union soldiers back to health. She founded the American Red Cross in 1881 and led the organization for more than 20 years.

**THOMAS ALVA EDISON
(1847–1931)**

Thomas Edison developed the phonograph, the motion-picture camera, the electric light bulb, and hundreds of other inventions. He grew up in the Midwest but spent his most productive years in New Jersey, first at Menlo Park and then in West Orange. In 1954, the town of Menlo Park, where the inventor had built a laboratory, was renamed Edison in his honor.

WOODROW WILSON (1856–1924)

A Virginian by birth, Woodrow Wilson spent his college years at Princeton and served as president of the university from 1902 to 1910. After two years as governor of New Jersey, he won election in 1912 as the nation's 28th president. In that office, he helped to protect workers' rights and led the United States to victory in World War I.

BRUCE SPRINGSTEEN (1949–)

Singer, songwriter, and bandleader Bruce Springsteen was born in Long Branch, New Jersey, and grew up in Freehold. Known to his fans as "The Boss," he has become one of the world's most famous musicians. His albums include *Greetings from Asbury Park*, *Born to Run*, *Born in the U.S.A.*, and *The Rising*.

QUEEN LATIFAH (1970–)

The daughter of a schoolteacher and a police officer, Dana Elaine Owens grew up in Newark. She first achieved success as a rapper using the stage name Queen Latifah. Later, she became one of Hollywood's top stars, appearing in such films as *Chicago* and *Bringing Down the House*. Queen Latifah also hosted her own talk show on television.

Bill Bradley (1943–) excelled in both sports and politics. He starred in basketball for Princeton University, on the U.S. Olympic team, and with the New York Knicks of the National Basketball Association. Later, he represented New Jersey for 18 years in the U.S. Senate.

Jon Stewart (1962–) was originally named Jonathan Stuart Leibowitz and grew up in Lawrenceville, New Jersey. The comedian hosts *The Daily Show* on national television.

Population

Nearly 8.8 million people lived in New Jersey at the time of the 2010 Census, making it the nation's 11th most populous state. New Jersey has the highest **population density** of any state in the United States, with more than 1,180 people per square mile of land area. The state's population density is more than 13 times that of the United States as a whole.

More than 90 percent of New Jersey residents live in urban areas. Much of the population lives in the northeastern part of the state, near New York City. New Jersey's four largest cities are Newark, Jersey City, Paterson, and Elizabeth. All four lie across the Hudson River from New York City.

New Jersey Population 1950–2010

Although New Jersey's population increased by 4.5 percent between 2000 and 2010, this rate of increase was less than half of the national average. What are some reasons why New Jersey grew more slowly than other states?

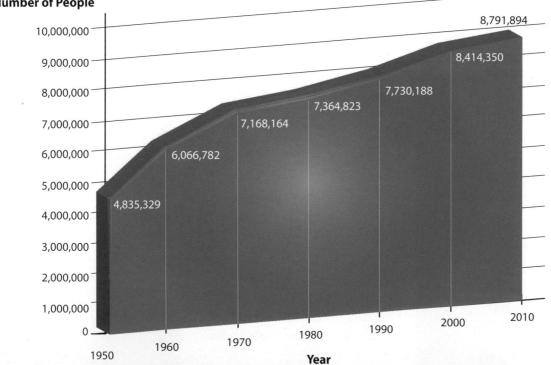

Number of People

- 4,835,329
- 6,066,782
- 7,168,164
- 7,364,823
- 7,730,188
- 8,414,350
- 8,791,894

Year: 1950, 1960, 1970, 1980, 1990, 2000, 2010

About 145,000 people live in Paterson, the third-largest city in New Jersey. A section of the city has been designated as a national historic district.

Close to New York City and home to more than 240,000 people, Jersey City has become a major financial center.

Politics and Government

Many years ago, only New Jerseyans who owned land could hold positions in government. These people were called freeholders. The landholding requirement is long gone, but New Jersey's counties are still run by groups of officials called boards of freeholders. Members of these boards are elected to three-year terms.

The state government consists of three branches. They are the executive, the legislative, and the judicial branches. The governor, who is elected to a four-year term, leads the executive branch. Unlike many other states, New Jersey does not have a lieutenant governor.

Chris Christie, a Republican, won election to a four-year term as state governor in November 2009.

Grover Cleveland, who served two separate terms as U.S. president, was born in New Jersey.

New Jersey does not have an official state song. Many songs have been proposed for the honor, including Bruce Springsteen's "Born to Run." At various times, the state legislature has given its approval to "I'm from New Jersey," with words and music by Red Mascara of Phillipsburg.

Here is an excerpt from the song:

*I'M FROM NEW JERSEY and
   I'm proud about it,
   I love the Garden State.
I'M FROM NEW JERSEY and
   I want to shout it, I think
   it's simply great.
All of the other states
   throughout the nation may
   mean a lot to some;
But I wouldn't want another,
Jersey is like no other, I'm glad
   that's where I'm from.*

The legislative branch makes the laws. The two houses of the legislature are the Senate, which has 40 members, and the General Assembly, which has 80 members. Senators serve four-year terms, except at the start of each decade, when all senators hold office for only two years. This system is known as the "2-4-4" cycle. All Assembly members serve two-year terms.

A Supreme Court heads New Jersey's judicial branch. There are also county, municipal, appeals, and tax courts. The New Jersey Supreme Court consists of a chief justice and six associate judges. The governor appoints the members of the court, but they do not take office until confirmed by the state Senate.

Cultural Groups

New Jersey is home to a wide range of cultural groups. It was the site of the first American Indian reservation, which was created in 1758 at the site of present-day Indian Mills in Burlington County. Early European settlers from England, Sweden, and the Netherlands were joined, particularly after the Civil War, by immigrants from Germany and Ireland. In the 20th century, many immigrants also came from Southern and Eastern Europe, particularly Italy. Today many of their descendants still live in the New Jersey area.

More than 1 million Hispanic Americans live in New Jersey. Latinos celebrate their culture during Hispanic Heritage Month, which runs from September 15 to October 15 each year. In the first week of September, Atlantic City hosts the Festival Latino-Americano, which showcases musicians playing Latin jazz and salsa. Dancers are also on hand to demonstrate their traditional skills and costumes.

The New Jersey Nets basketball team honors the state's Hispanic heritage by sponsoring an annual Latin Night.

African Americans have played an important role in New Jersey's history. Before the Civil War, some of the state's churches and businesses helped escaped slaves traveling north to freedom on the **Underground Railroad**. In 1926, Lawnside became the state's first self-governing African American community. The Afro-American Historical Society Museum, in Jersey City, has exhibits on the life and history of African Americans in the state.

In Atlantic City, a site that is popularly called Chicken Bone Beach was the only city beach that African Americans were allowed to use from 1900 to the 1950s. Although the beach developed as a result of racial **segregation**, it came to represent African American unity and has been made into a historic site. The beach hosted large celebrations with live jazz and picnic lunches. The beach got its name from the remains of pan-fried chicken lunches that were eaten there.

Harriet Tubman, a fighter for African American rights, worked in the 1850s at a Cape May hotel. She used her earnings to finance her anti-slavery activities.

I DIDN'T KNOW THAT!

Many well-known African American entertainers have grown up in New Jersey. Among them are Sarah Vaughan, a talented jazz singer, and Whitney Houston, a world-famous popular singer. Hip-hop artist Lauryn Hill achieved stardom both with the group the Fugees and as a solo performer.

The Powhatan Renape Nation, in Burlington County, educates people about the beliefs, traditions, and culture of the area's American Indians.

The Peter Mott House in Lawnside, built in the mid-1800s, was once a station on the Underground Railroad. It is now a museum.

Hackensack is the site of one of the most important jazz-recording studios of all time. Rudy Van Gelder set up a studio in his parents' living room and went on to record the sounds of such jazz greats as Miles Davis and John Coltrane.

Arts and Entertainment

For fans of music and the arts, New Jersey has numerous theaters, museums, concert halls, and opera houses. The New Jersey Performing Arts Center, located in Newark, is among the largest arts centers in the country. Opened in 1997, the center is home to the New Jersey Symphony Orchestra, which entertains listeners with the sounds of classical music. Other centers for the performing arts include the State Theater in New Brunswick, the McCarter Theater in Princeton, and the Count Basie Theater in Red Bank. The PNC Arts Center in Holmdel presents a summer concert series featuring pop music performers.

Magician David Copperfield was born in Metuchen. He was admitted into the Society of American Magicians at age 12 and taught magic at New York University by the time he was 16. Since then, Copperfield has performed many amazing tricks, such as escaping from a flaming raft over Niagara Falls and walking through the Great Wall of China.

Master magician David Copperfield has been honored as a Living Legend by the U.S. Library of Congress.

Many notable musicians, performers, and writers have called New Jersey home. The singer Frank Sinatra was born in Hoboken in 1915. Sinatra charmed the world with his renditions of jazz ballads and show tunes, including "New York, New York." Paul Simon, Bruce Springsteen, Jon Bon Jovi, and rapper and actor Ice-T also come from the state.

Meryl Streep, Jack Nicholson, and Michael Douglas are Hollywood stars who grew up in New Jersey and have won Academy Awards for best actress or actor. Among the other actors and comics born in the state are Jerry Lewis, Joe Pesci, Danny DeVito, and the comedy team of Bud Abbott and Lou Costello.

Famous writers born in or associated with New Jersey include the poets Joyce Kilmer, Walt Whitman, and William Carlos Williams and the novelists Norman Mailer, Philip Roth, Stephen Crane, Toni Morrison, and Judy Blume. Blume has written many humorous and honest novels for young people, including *Are You There God?*, *It's Me, Margaret* and *Otherwise Known as Sheila the Great*.

Rock star Jon Bon Jovi is a native of Perth Amboy.

At the Walt Whitman House in Camden, visitors can view some of the poet's early letters and poems as well as an early photo of Whitman from 1848.

The New Jersey State Museum in Trenton features a planetarium. The museum, which opened in 1895, also houses art, science, and history exhibits.

Acclaimed for her novel *Beloved*, Toni Morrison was a Princeton University professor from 1989 to 2006.

Sports

New Jersey has much to offer fans of professional sports. Several pro teams play their games at the Meadowlands Sports Complex in East Rutherford. The complex includes three major facilities. It has a horse-racing track that hosts the Hambletonian, one of harness racing's most important annual events. The Meadowlands also contains New Meadowlands Stadium, home of the New York Giants and the New York Jets of the National Football League, and the Izod Center, which offers a varied calendar of sports and arts events. The New Jersey Devils of the National Hockey League and the New Jersey Nets of the National Basketball Association play at the Prudential Center in Newark. Red Bull Arena in Harrison is the home of the Red Bulls of Major League Soccer.

Quarterbacked by Mark Sanchez, the New York Jets began playing their home games at New Meadowlands Stadium in 2010.

The Atlantic Ocean is a popular destination for swimmers and boaters. Every year, swimmers brave the chilly ocean waters to take part in Atlantic City's Around the Island Marathon Swim. The Atlantic provides a wide variety of fish to catch. Fishing in New Jersey streams and rivers is also popular.

For those who prefer to stay on land, New Jersey's golf courses and ski areas provide plenty of outdoor recreation. New Jersey is also a great place for horse lovers. The state is home to the U.S. Equestrian Team, based in Gladstone. Each June, spectators can watch the nation's best horse riders at Gladstone's Festival of Champions.

The Seton Hall and Rutgers women's basketball teams represent New Jersey in the Big East Conference.

Famous athletes from New Jersey include track-and-field star Carl Lewis, skater Dick Button, basketball players Shaquille O'Neal and Rick Barry, tennis player Michael Chang, baseball star Derek Jeter, boxer Jersey Joe Walcott, and football player Franco Harris. Football coach Amos Alonzo Stagg also came from the Garden State.

Hoboken hosted the first organized baseball game in 1846. Baseball historians refer to the event as "the day baseball was born." The historic game was held at Elysian Fields.

The first pro basketball game was played in Trenton in 1896.

In 1869, New Brunswick hosted the first intercollegiate football game, between Rutgers and Princeton.

In the annual Polar Bear Plunge, swimmers raise money for charity by braving frigid ocean waters each February at Sea Isle.

National Averages Comparison

The United States is a federal republic, consisting of fifty states and the District of Columbia. Alaska and Hawai'i are the only non-contiguous, or non-touching, states in the nation. Today, the United States of America is the third-largest country in the world in population. The United States Census Bureau takes a census, or count of all the people, every ten years. It also regularly collects other kinds of data about the population and the economy. How does New Jersey compare to the national average?

Comparison Chart

United States 2010 Census Data *	USA	New Jersey
Admission to Union	NA	December 18, 1787
Land Area (in square miles)	3,537,438.44	7,417.34
Population Total	308,745,538	8,791,894
Population Density (people per square mile)	87.28	1,185.32
Population Percentage Change (April 1, 2000, to April 1, 2010)	9.7%	4.5%
White Persons (percent)	72.4%	68.6%
Black Persons (percent)	12.6%	13.7%
American Indian and Alaska Native Persons (percent)	0.9%	0.3%
Asian Persons (percent)	4.8%	8.3%
Native Hawaiian and Other Pacific Islander Persons (percent)	0.2%	—
Some Other Race (percent)	6.2%	6.4%
Persons Reporting Two or More Races (percent)	2.9%	2.7%
Persons of Hispanic or Latino Origin (percent)	16.3%	17.7%
Not of Hispanic or Latino Origin (percent)	83.7%	82.3%
Median Household Income	$52,029	$70,347
Percentage of People Age 25 or Over Who Have Graduated from High School	80.4%	82.1%

*All figures are based on the 2010 United States Census, with the exception of the last two items.

How to Improve My Community

Strong communities make strong states. Think about what features are important in your community. What do you value? Education? Health? Forests? Safety? Beautiful spaces? Government works to help citizens create ideal living conditions that are fair to all by providing services in communities. Consider what changes you could make in your community. How would they improve your state as a whole? Using this concept web as a guide, write a report that outlines the features you think are most important in your community and what improvements could be made. A strong state needs strong communities.

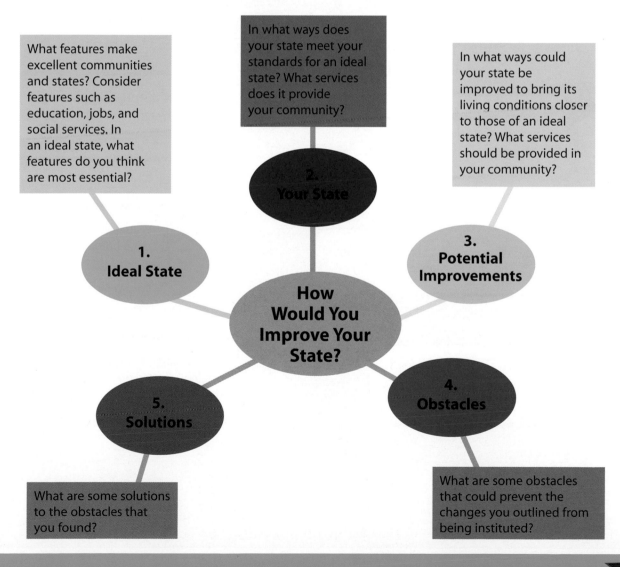

What features make excellent communities and states? Consider features such as education, jobs, and social services. In an ideal state, what features do you think are most essential?

In what ways does your state meet your standards for an ideal state? What services does it provide your community?

In what ways could your state be improved to bring its living conditions closer to those of an ideal state? What services should be provided in your community?

**2.
Your State**

**1.
Ideal State**

**3.
Potential
Improvements**

**How
Would You
Improve Your
State?**

**5.
Solutions**

**4.
Obstacles**

What are some solutions to the obstacles that you found?

What are some obstacles that could prevent the changes you outlined from being instituted?

Think about these questions and then use your research skills to find the answers and learn more fascinating facts about New Jersey. A teacher, librarian, or parent may be able to help you locate the best sources to use in your research.

1 What was Elizabeth Lee known for?

2 What mythical monster is said to live in New Jersey's Pine Barrens?

3 What craft was first launched in the Passaic River in 1878?

4 What famous candy was first sold in the 1880s in Atlantic City?

5 What flying object spooked the residents of Totowa in 1908?

6 How did a "frog" help end a bitter battle between two New Jersey railroad companies in the 1870s?

7 Would it be difficult to get a burger and fries in New Jersey?

8 What board game was originally based on street names in Atlantic City?

Words to Know

archaeologists: scientists who study early peoples through artifacts and remains

commuters: people who travel to and from their jobs, usually by car or train

descendants: relatives

endangered species: a kind of animal or plant that is in danger of completely dying out

immunity: natural defenses against disease

industrialization: the introduction of manufacturing industries to an area

innovation: the act of creating or introducing something new

navigator: a skilled person who directs a moving craft, such as a ship or plane, to its destination

persecuted: to be harassed because of one's religion, race, or beliefs

pharmaceuticals: medicines used to cure sickness and disease

population density: the average number of people per unit of area

prehistoric: the period before written history began

proprietors: owners of colonies in North America

ratify: to approve formally

segregation: forcing separation and restrictions based on race

Underground Railroad: a system for helping slaves escape

urbanized: resembling a modern city with housing, industries, roads, and a dense population

Index

Log on to www.av2books.com

AV² by Weigl brings you media enhanced books that support active learning. Go to www.av2books.com, and enter the special code found on page 2 of this book. You will gain access to enriched and enhanced content that supplements and complements this book. Content includes video, audio, web links, quizzes, a slide show, and activities.

Audio
Listen to sections of the book read aloud.

Video
Watch informative video clips.

Embedded Weblinks
Gain additional information for research.

Try This!
Complete activities and hands-on experiments.

WHAT'S ONLINE?

Try This!	Embedded Weblinks	Video	EXTRA FEATURES
Test your knowledge of the state in a mapping activity.	Discover more attractions in New Jersey.	Watch a video introduction to New Jersey.	**Audio** Listen to sections of the book read aloud.
Find out more about precipitation in your city.	Learn more about the history of the state.	Watch a video about the features of the state.	**Key Words** Study vocabulary, and complete a matching word activity.
Plan what attractions you would like to visit in the state.	Learn the full lyrics of the state song.		**Slide Show** View images and captions, and prepare a presentation.
Learn more about the early natural resources of the state.			
Write a biography about a notable resident of New Jersey.			**Quizzes** Test your knowledge.
Complete an educational census activity.			

AV² was built to bridge the gap between print and digital. We encourage you to tell us what you like and what you want to see in the future.

Sign up to be an AV² Ambassador at www.av2books.com/ambassador.